GW00362052

SEASONS' BEAUTY

Edited by

Steph Park-Pirie

First published in Great Britain in 2004 by
POETRY NOW
Remus House,
Coltsfoot Drive,
Peterborough, PE2 9JX
Telephone (01733) 898101
Fax (01733) 313524

All Rights Reserved

Copyright Contributors 2004

SB ISBN 1 84460 797 6

FOREWORD

Although we are a nation of poets we are accused of not reading poetry, or buying poetry books. After many years of listening to the incessant gripes of poetry publishers, I can only assume that the books they publish, in general, are books that most people do not want to read.

Poetry should not be obscure, introverted, and as cryptic as a crossword puzzle: it is the poet's duty to reach out and embrace the world.

The world owes the poet nothing and we should not be expected to dig and delve into a rambling discourse searching for some inner meaning.

The reason we write poetry (and almost all of us do) is because we want to communicate: an ideal; an idea; or a specific feeling. Poetry is as essential in communication, as a letter; a radio; a telephone, and the main criterion for selecting the poems in this anthology is very simple: they communicate.

CONTENTS

THE ARRIVAL OF THE SPRING

The awakening countryside welcomes the arrival of the spring
Those beautiful songbirds greet the sun when they sing
Those beautiful swans are busy making their reed nests
The sun awakens the trees from their long winter's rest.

The woodlands have been sleeping through those cold winter months
Those migrating birds are slowly returning from the south
The hunting kestrels are hovering in the morning sky for their prey
Those small field mice are building their nests out of hay.

In the stone cow shed, an expecting mother waiting its calf's birth
It's Mother Nature's gift, the awakening spring has returned to Earth
The sweet morning rain has now washed the earth from its winter rest
Then soon the young are being born in burrows and treetop nests.

Then the blossoms will appear so beautiful as they dress the trees
The wood hives are humming the sweet songs of honey bees
The farmyard animals, their bellowing voices to greet the dawn
Then across the countryside, the woodlands welcome the newly-born.

When you see the daisies and the clover in the meadow's grass
The dark nights of winter have departed and spring has arrived at last
The yellow cowslips and the catkins are in their crowing glory
This season of spring can always tell a beautiful new story.

J F Grainger

WINTER BOLDLY BARE

I just stare
At winter boldly bare.
The stoic stark,
The early drab dark,
With less light to play
From the lower sun day.

My hopes are churning,
I am so yearning
For the winter white,
To be where the ice crystals shine beauty bright.
To wrap warm in woolly hat, gloves and scarf,
Pull on long boots,
Have a wild winter laugh.

Winter boldly bare
Has me in desolate despair.
Just to touch the frosty flakes cold,
To hear the sagas by the flickering fire told,
To sip the mulled wine, feel all aglow,
Oh! I want to visit winter's white snow,
Feel it falling powdery on my lashes,
Whirling, dancing, be where it softly crashes.

I've given sparkling silver, dreaming tears,
To find the canvas I've painted for years.
That hot breath on ultra-cold air,
It is there, somewhere.
As I hum a hopeful prayer,
I just stare,
At winter boldly bare.

Carol Ann Darling

The Sweetness Of Spring

Welcome the sweetness
Of this season, spring.
Milder, longer days,
Losing winter's sting.

Meek lambs are skipping,
Nimble, spry birds sing,
A time of rebirth,
What Mother Nature brings.

Elegant dancing daffodils,
Each wears a gold crown.
Catkins shake their tails,
Earth wears a primrose gown.

Eggs hidden in nests,
Purple violets on the dell,
Poised, delicate apple blossom,
Ambrosial, fragrant smell.

Peep daisies in the meadows,
Woolly clouds white,
A gaily dressed rainbow
On the horizon in sight.

Cute bob-tailed rabbits,
Frolic, play all day,
Hardly woken from sleep,
Hedgerow buds so gay.

Kissed cowslips grow,
Treasures so rare,
For everyone on Earth,
Sweet spring to share.

Patricia Carter

SPRING

Now that spring is here,
Flowers reach up to the sun
And God's hand touches every one.
Rain to quench their thirst,
Soon beauty will burst,
All of summer long.

David A Bray

BREAKFAST MENU

Summer shoots
Fresh spring green.
Old winter leaves
Still autumn-toasted.
Smears of amber marmalade
Nature spread.
Bronzed, waving in the sun
Buttered daffodils.
Bees wax and wane
Glistening, dancing in the rain.

Trees - barking
Their trunks, drunk
As on summer wine
Cones lick the cool chocolate earth.
Branches break
Milking sap.
Petals peeling
Fall
Sugaring
Brown coffee roasted soil.

Marilyn Hodgson

LOOKING BACK ON WINTERS

When I look back on winter times
I remember when everything was fine
I would look forward to the snow
Sometimes it was so cold my nose would glow
And we would make a snowman and dress him up
Using coal, and a carrot, and other stuff
I felt sad seeing the trees with their branches bare
But knew in the spring new leaves would be there
That was then, but this is now
And winters don't seem the same somehow
Now I dread the thought of snow and ice
And now I no longer think it is nice
As I wait and wonder if I will get a bus
I wish it was not me, but still us
Yes winters used to be such fun
Now I'm glad when they are over and done.

Eileen Kyte

A Year Observed

Lighter nights and fluorescent sights
Of flowers waiting to bloom
A silent cry of joy
For the blaze of colour soon

Bright with blue
Cut grass and jet streams
Children playing too,
Swallows rule the sky
And your dreams with them up high

Rich and still
The ghost of summer
In the image of mists
The forest breathes a sigh
And its tears seem happy where they lie

Two-tone days of grey and white
Sweet and sleepy nights way out of sight
A warm open fire with a life of desire
At Christmas we sing
It'll soon be spring.

Steve Roberts

KING OF ICE

(A tribute to Derek Brockway, weatherman)

Winter is here
With daylight cheer
The days are so cold
But so clear.
The mountains are
Surrounded in a blanket
Jack frost nips your toes
Biting at your eyes and nose.
Winter is here
Coal fires are lit
The valley is white below
Surrounded by a white throw.
The sun has lost its warmth
Christmas is over for another year
Jack Frost is still here
He surrounds you with his
Cloak of ice.
We look to summer
With no fear
Winter has been and gone.
It won't be missed by anyone.

S I Groves

A SUMMER'S DAY

A summer's day or dead of night
A bumblebee or bird in flight
The crested tide upon the sand
Two hearts in love stroll hand in hand

The autumn leaves of golden brown
A quiet place away from town
A leafy lane of bronze and gold
Stone-built cottages ages old

The rolling hills that have through time
Endured nature in her prime
The limestone crags that stand so proud
The weekend climbers well endowed

The sound of laughter on the pier
The summer show out on its rear
The best in life may not be free
But memories are what maketh to me.

Bilbo

AUTUMN ON THE GREEN

A harvest sun in the sky,
The Essex countryside takes a sigh,
Golden chestnuts' leaves drop and die,
Reddish nuts on the ground lie,
Grey squirrels scamper about,
Looking for a place to hibernate,
Whilst birds congregate, ready to migrate.
The air is filled with the smells of autumn.
Autumn on the green.
Bells ringing in the church tower,
The noise of the wind is nature's choir.
Burning up of allotment fires.
Sure the earth will awake from winter.
In the spring it will bloom once more.

B G Clarke

AUTUMN LEAVES

They dance in the woods,
They go merrily floating down the road
In many shades of brown, so good!
A pleasing sight you won't forget,
Evergreens stand still, as yet.
Those who doubt to see God's great powers
As He transforms the green leaves into brown,
This is proof that we all fade away, as a leaf,
To be reborn again, whosoever believes in Him,
Will reap, and be in His keep.

Sammy Michael Davis

SPRING'S AMOUR

Daffodils that wave and call
as spring is heralded in once more.
Just the fragrance on the bough
that makes us feel
much life reborn.

Through winter's dead and darkened touch,
we all hope for snowdrops peep.
Of battered winds at headlands reach
and the bareness of landscape's gaze,
may calmness fall by April's hand.

Birdsong of such delight,
to make free with
twig and moss;
for nests to build,
within eggs that lay,
as young do hatch
and swiftly grow.

Much beauty found in tulips' shade
of colours found all around.
Let earth's powers restore such growth,
for each new lightened day
be spring's embrace
that we may share.

G E Fitzjohn

So Sublime!

Autumn is such a lovely time.
It is so sublime!
Mellow fruitfulness that melts
And ripens and has felt
The autumn chill at night.
It rises to the height.
Rich colours of browns and reds.
The dahlias lift their heads.
Autumn is such a lovely time.
It is above all sublime!

I T Hoggan

ODE TO AUTUMN

Flowers are losing their summer bloom,
Leaves are turning yellow, gold, and brown,
Gently they flutter down to the ground
Autumn has really arrived here now.
Soon the long summer evenings will be a dream
As they shorten to emerge with winter's theme
Snow and frost will cover the earth and trees
No more to hear soft buzzing of bees.
Instead we will see robin, an inquisitive bird,
Sitting on our window sills waiting to be fed
People rubbing their hands, stamping their feet
To keep the circulation going, keep in the heat.
Occasionally one hears the calling of rooks
Children in school pouring of their books
Looking out of the window now and then
Thinking of happy summer days.
Still seasons come and go
We have got one season that makes us glow
With happiness and merriment too.
Christmas, a lovely season full of good cheer
With the giving of presents to girls and boys
Cheeks all aglow, playing with their toys
Old folk sitting by the fire so bright
Lamps lit up with golden light.
We miss summer and autumn too
But the winter season I love so much
Christmas is magic at a touch.
So be of good cheer, grown-ups and kids
Although the seasons come and go
They all play their part as seasons come and go.

Irene Hartley

AUTUMN

Autumn comes around again
With shorter days and welcome rain
After the heat of the summer sun
Many plants, for this year, are done.

The leaves are falling from the trees,
Scattered around by the freshening breeze.
Beautiful colours, gold, orange and red,
My feet make them crunch as on them I tread.

The corn and fruits are harvested now
Apples, pears, plums, picked from the bough,
Put into store for the winter to come,
For us to enjoy when work is done.

So, once again autumn is here,
Another season in the changing year,
All created by our God above
Who keeps this world a-turning with His unfailing love.

V Hankins

ASPECTS OF AUTUMN

The leaves of autumn lay in swathes beneath the trees,
Swirling colourfully and fitfully in the chilly breeze.
Shades of green, brown, red and gold
Reveal the colours the branches could not hold.

The heavy showers and winds that bluster
Strip the trees of many a leafy cluster.
Finally the trees are practically bared
With but a few evergreens that are spared.

The cotton wool mist hugs the ground
As it gently moves forward without a sound.
Its chilly touch seeps gradually into your bones,
Bring forth soft whimpering moans.

Dusk arrives in late afternoon
And daylight vanishes all too soon.
When workers leave for home at night
It's the streetlight, and not their outlooks, which are bright.

Summer has now run its course
And we've reached the interval before we feel winter's force.
A time to recollect holidays and summer treats,
A time to prepare for our winter retreats.

Allen Jessop

AUTUMNAL PREFERENCES

The autumn colours magnetise,
And pens will share what fills our eyes.
The words will also capture, share,
The frosted grass, and breath-filled air.

The dark'ing nights, so clear, frosted,
Will strengthen as the sun's accosted.
The festivals for harvest Bloom,
Will leave the churches with no room.

Whilst shortly followed witches' pots,
Will bubble as the fallen rots.
Then fireworks will bring us bright,
Upon late autumn's frosting night.

And yet whilst all appeals to thee,
The scents of autumn fulfil me.
Like damp and musty scent-filled land,
Somehow holds my nose in command.

But most of all the oak tree leaves,
Will smoulder as my soul perceives
That autumn now is mine to taste,
And not a moment shall I waste.

Sid de Knees

AUTUMN VARIETY

Seasonal change,
Quicksilvered moods,
Clothes,
The autumn collection.

Tints of autumn,
Leaves, red, gold, brown,
Fruit,
Harvested perfection.

Scarlet rose hips,
Poppies glowing,
Red,
Dates of recollection.

Nocturnal sight,
Bright moon at night,
Strange
Tales of things mortals shun.

Lights, theatres, bars,
First frosts showing,
'Proms',
Bonfires, fireworks like stars.

Kathleen M Scatchard

WILD FLOWER

Fair wild flowers of multicolour,
Your fragrance as sweet as a child's
Sweet demeanour.

You grow beneath the yellow leaves' fall,
Oh carrier of life for insects to crawl.
The river flows so near to your edge,
To bring you life, for its soul's sacred pledge.

The sun filters through to give you your strength,
To dance in the wind, and multiply in length.
You spread your beauty for all to see,
So the woods give our race a place to be.

Thank you nature for showing us your story,
It's perfect in form and should take all the glory.
Without your presence life would be much less,
Without your care, life would be in a mess.

Ricky N Lock

A DAY IN JUNE

June days have come
once more . . .
Summer Surprises
are in store . . .
Perfect days,
so lush and fair . . .
A day in June,
in a month so rare . . .

Carol Olson

SPRING IN ARGYLL

Land of silver showers and fleeting rainbows,
Hills of purple - bracken gold and green,
Turquoise sea reflecting springtime heavens,
Shimmering sun upon the mist-blue scene.
Sting-cold, ice-pure tides from rolling oceans,
Hidden glens, and rivers rushing free.
This, the world's one corner 'bove all others
Which ever holds a welcome smile for me.

F M Reed

SPRING SONG

Children of the spring, arise,
your time has come to call
the sleeping from their winter graves,
the dead world to enthral.

Dance upon the springtime green,
spread the primrose gold.
Flit your hope through weary minds,
make your budding hold.

Sing your promise to each heart,
lift each darkened mind.
Coax stern winter, through your smiles,
to leave his cares behind.

Christala Rosina

My Summer Fled

Dove of peace hovered at your bed
To escort you into unknown,
Sky darkened as my summer fled.

Your spirit flew to secret stead,
I stood thunderstruck and alone,
Dove of peace hovered at your bed.

Underfoot ground opened widespread,
Dread gripped fearing lives overthrown,
Sky darkened as my summer fled.

Meaningful words at end unsaid,
You departed before signs shown,
Dove of peace hovered at your bed.

Erudite you have winged ahead,
Shall watch seeds of knowledge you've sown,
Sky darkened as my summer fled.

Hear anecdotes about you spread,
Brightening days of monotone,
Dove of peace hovered at your bed,
Sky darkened as my summer fled.

Hilary Jill Robson

A TIME OF DESPAIR FOR MANY

It is a season of bleakness, a time that brings great gloom
For many creatures in the wild, it enshrouds them in its tomb
And the frail and elderly fear this time, it reaches out each day
The grim reaper leaving its calling card, seeking to take them away.

Jack Frost drops his visiting card, for at least three months he calls
Frustrated motorists swear in anger, when the car engine stalls
The rape and pillaging of God's own earth, is a devastating sight
                                                    to behold
Causing devastation across this pleasant land, once it takes its hold.

Fields that once yielded corn and barley, now lay bitter and frozen hard
Trees and bushes, along country roads, stand quietly, battle scarred
It makes its presence known in other ways, with dark and dismal nights
Temperatures drop, the heating goes on, heavy bills, as it cruelly bites.

Dark swirling clouds drift overhead, swept on by a vengeful broom
Nowt else to do but watch the television, inside a heated room
Freezing nights kill off many birds, all wildlife has to fight
When heavy snowfalls settle, they battle with all of their might.

They do not have the warm comforts, that we are able to use
Nor are there plenty of blankets, from which they are able to choose
Struggling against the elements, on these many bitter, frozen days
They combat these difficult conditions, in their tried and trusted ways.

Two thirds of December gone, we find the shortest day of the year
And gradually, but very slowly, the dark, early nights seem to disappear
Brighter mornings find their way in, heralding the coming of the spring
And this signifies the brightness and beauty, of every living thing.

And as this season passes by, of which we have had our fill
A hazy sun rises on the horizon, helping to ward off the chill
People appear more cheerful, with the ending of a time so bleak
A time that is always dangerous, to our older citizens and the weak.

And so we look forward to the ending of the many early nights of dark
Anticipating with eagerness the morning songs of the early rising lark.

B W Ballard

LAST WEEK IN AUGUST

August is not trivial.
She is the summer's pain
in heat and rain.
Her heart is in
the burning grass.
Trees that fade.
She is a broom,
a hospital of dying leaves.
Children start school again
and look for air-conditioned rooms.
They long for the sweet grass of summer.
Poets have dreams before they turn her off.
August is not trivial.

Marion Schoeberlein

WINTER THROES

In the throes of winter
Frosts, cold, ice and snow
That was winter in the past.
Now the ozone layer has gone,
Maybe snow in February,
Or once as I've said before,
Weather seems so behind.
England's Christmas gets snow no more.

Michael D Bedford

THE WONDER OF SPRING

Spring's here, gardens, plush luscious green
Dewdrops kiss baby crocuses, dazzle the springtime scene
Beautiful borders, little snowdrops, gardens' sweet delight
Blue coral skies, nature performs, amazing delicate sight.
Tulips caress swaying daffodils, nature springs supreme
Sunshine breaks through, vanishing snow left gleaming
Winter woodlands left barren, nature foliage naked trees
Nature creates these wonders, with such graceful ease
Clumping pansies, scented wallflowers, complete delightful splash
Coloured, splendid roses, ever climbing, final dash
Wonderful sounds hum, spring's birds, insects, bees,
Enter refreshing, renewing season's balmy breeze
Abundant fragrance adorns garden's springtime face
Baby lambs jump and skip, butterflies chase
Breezes blow blossoms' canopy, adorable white
Sky brings new meaning, clouds, soft, fluffy, light
Dancing spring flowers, treasured gardens' lace
Oh heavenly garden, framed by spring's fair grace.

Ann Hathaway

AUTUMN

Autumn's here again at last, when the leaves go flying past,
Brought down by the winds and rain, blown into the gutters and drains,
Never more to grace the trees, or to flutter in the breeze.
Once they were of colours bright, oranges, reds and golds,
Now they fall upon the ground, shrivelled up and old.
But we can remember how proud they once were,
Talking to the passing breeze, and the birds on wing,
Singing as they gently swayed, like feathers on a swing.
As they fall to earth to die, they gaze up into the sky,
Knowing that again next year, all their offspring will appear
To carry on this wonderful scheme as we see another spring.

Dorothy Brown

SWEET ROBIN

Little robin hides inside a sweet green swathe
A phantom that quickly appears from his hideaway haze
His eyes alight, his beak upright
As he listens to the melodic memory of the wintry wind
So prim and proper is your show
Your red breast is aglow
Alight and moving like lava of the volcano
Darting hither, sliding whither
Random is the movement has he dots and dashes around
For his Christmas meal
A small grain here
A tasty morsel there
After feed, sleepy he looks, as he blows out his chest
Leaning onto a holly bough
The frost still keen and crisp at his feet
The winter snow is now the artist
Carving, drawing, scouring
A faint line, a bold line, our robin joins the picture
As he skates onto the scene
Adding a harvest of footprint textures to the winter machine
As the dusk appears, little robin is stood still
He lazily retreats and blends back to nature
So still, so beautiful
We look away to the fireplace shelf and remember this vision
We imprint it on the Christmas card
That becomes our lasting memory
The red glow of the fire, his lasting warmth
Goodnight till tomorrow
Sweet robin.

Steve Powell

PORTENT

Harsh white muslin
will soon return
to drape the hill
and sparkle with
devilish glee in the
ageing summer sun
which rises with
increasing lethargy.

The noon of summer
was so brief . . .
and now;
sunset takes us unaware
and dawn is far away.

Mornings can be disturbed
to see the sun
restrained by leaden cloud
when breezes laze
in the doldrums
and take no heed
of the sun's misery.

Surely . . .
spring will return?
Meanwhile . . .
autumn's gorgeous cloak
is our cushion, until
the hard hand of winter
descends to crush the spirit.

Kinsman Clive

THOUGHTS ON WINTER

Winter is the time I feel blue,
Do other people feel that too?

I often wish I could hide away,
Or travel to Australia today.

My brain is in a sorry state
And I'd like to hibernate.

The weather is damp and cold,
Then viruses start to take hold.

It's hard to get out of bed,
I can't face the day ahead.

After Christmas things are bleak,
Depression is at its peak.

I pray for March to come along,
So I can hear joyful birdsong.

Daffodils push through the earth,
Nature begins its rebirth.

Branches dress up in green sleeves,
As trees begin to sprout new leaves.

Now the sun peeps out at last,
Yes, I think old winter's past.

Rosemary Davies

WINTER PRISMS

Icicles hang like crystal prisms
From every branch of all the trees.
As if each tiny crystal raindrop
Hangs suspended in mid-air freeze.
Snow-capped trees caught by breezes,
Crystals all collide together.
Sunlight glitters on the snowdrifts
In this crisp, clear winter weather.

Tinkling prisms making music,
Composing nature's melodies.
Snowflakes drifting down in showers,
Blown in flurries by the breeze.
Sunlight shining through each crystal,
Dancing rainbows on the snow.
A moving kaleidoscope of colours
And music, nature's winter show.

Patricia Draper

AUTUMNAL THOUGHT

Superabundance of our joys,
sublimity
in summer;
newcomer
(mores the pity),
September, punctual, annoys.

A familiar theme transmutes;
insipid light's
invasion
a change invites
occasion
warrants, along with amber fruits.

Simultaneously coral
and subtle mauve
merge with sound,
depth profound;
desires behove
themselves to blend, their quarrel

quelled, music making itself clear
in welcome notes,
harvests reap;
slowly creep
the dust motes
of winter solstice drawing near.

Ghostly and garlanded is gone
a dream we dreamt
of laughter
for after
sad leaves unkempt,
bronzed, vacate trees they flourished on.

Rumbustious the August chord;
long wild phase's
cavalcade
starts to fade.
Then erases
yellow glare, sienna overlord.

Ruth Daviat

SOUNDS OF SUMMER

The drowsy hum of bees
Seeking the flowers' golden store
Of delicate-scented nectar.

The not so welcome drone of wasps,
Those stripy stinging insects
Sated with their sugary food.

The intermittent call of cuckoo,
Sure sign that summer days are here
Until he flies away.

Cooing of wood pigeons, less melodious collared doves,
And raucous cries of rooks and crows,
Predators of baby birds.

The cheeping of perky sparrows in the hedgerows,
The glorious song of blackbird perched on high
Upon a green-leaved branch.

More mundane sounds are heard in gardens all around
Where lawns industriously are mown
And spades dig deep into the earth.

These sounds so magical in summer sun
Are much more difficult to hear these days
When overlaid by strident noise.

The constant roar of traffic on the roads
And high up in the clear blue sky,
Engines of aircraft, helicopter blades.

The blare of radios and TVs
Issuing from windows open in the heat,
The constant ring of mobile phones.

Even the well-loved summer scents
Of garden flowers and new-mown grass
Are overlaid by toxic petrol fumes.

Alas, where are the sounds and scents of yesteryear?

Roma Davies

COLD

'Minus seven!' The very words strike cold,
As hoar frost daily grows on leafless trees;
This is the season dreaded by the old,
When biting, ice-toothed winds destroy their ease;
The wintry weather works its weary way
Into the body, the mind, the inmost soul;
The daylight shrinks, the spring is far away,
Will shivering bodies ever reach that goal?
Now warmth is hoarded even more than wealth,
As life becomes a fight to stay alive,
Each log, each coal a stepping stone to health,
A lifeline necessary to survive.
But spring will come and with it bring new life
To lighten hearts and take away all strife.

Bill Fletcher

BUS RIDE

December day
that tore the grey
with golden cold
makes brick walls gleam,
beam after beam
flash, hundredfold -

Teasing the eaves,
last yellow leaves
dance with delight,
this bright day's crown.
The road flows down
into wide white . . .

The city lies,
a lake of ice
in seeming calm;
the coal-black night
about to strike
is banned by charm.

The spell will shrink,
the night will sink
with numbing cold;
but candles throng
so small, so strong,
to gather gold.

Christina Egan

A HARD WINTER

The ponds were frozen solid, the frost had hardened the ground,
North wind blew the white snowflakes swirling all around,
Trees were bare, the leaves were gone, not one to be seen,
The drifting snow covered the meadows that had been so green,
Rabbits were in their burrows underneath the ground,
Game birds had taken shelter wherever it could be found,
No work could be done on the fields because they were so hard,
Cattle and sheep were bedded down with straw in the sheltered yard,
Still the farm workers had to work although they had to battle,
To feed the pigs, milk the cows, and take care of the cattle,
Getting to and from the farm was very hard to do,
As snowdrifts blocked the roads, they had to dig a pathway through,
When they arrived back home at night they were as tired as could be,
So with food on the table and a fire they were very glad to see,
Going to bed, they thanked the Lord for bringing them through that day,
And asked Him in His mercy to take the bad weather away,
When the sun shone after the clouds dispersed it was such a relief,
The change which followed in the spring was quite beyond belief.

Stan Gilbert

WINTERTIME

My aches and pains
Just play up more
The cold old blast
Comes in the door
I put on cardigans and socks
To try and warm me up
Cold toes
I do go out
No matter what
And battle on through
Wind and dust
The rain seems just
As bad for me
It makes me ache more
Hurts my knees
I try to reason with myself
It only lasts for
A small spell
And time as we all
Know it flies
The spring-like days
And bluer skies
So what the heck
If winter's bleak
It only lasts a few more weeks.

Jeanette Gaffney

ANOTHER SHORT WALK IN EARLY WINTER

The sky is even greyer,
The breeze is now a wind,
Cold but not yet bitter.
No clouds cry today,
But the air is damp,
Ferns lie brown and dark,
Seeking the earth, its warmth,
To live again.
The branches of the oaks
Click and clatter in the wind,
Shivering as if to say,
'Come back soon, sun, to keep me warm,
And I will greet you
With my colours of spring.'
But she does not come,
And it will be a while,
Before flowers bloom with nature's smile.

Ken Hunter

ODE TO AUTUMN

All safe and sound, spring's promise kept
From every tree
Leaves fall,
But still there is victory.

Colour above our heads, still on the paths we tread,
Will all our fears have such resolve.
Not war, but peace, unfold,
Still stands the tree.

Gold upon gold, but not for man's purse to hold.
Children unborn, not to see joy,
Whispering leaves, man's hard will,
Nature is free.

Over the earth, leaves scarlet and golden,
Hiding the man-made naked wounds,
With mercy unspoken,
His love to be.

Swiftly, as time goes, fall the leaves to the ground.
Problems that make no sense, no sound,
On coloured carpets, soft to the tread,
Answers for free.

Triumph to feel now, from colours ablaze,
Courage to make the right choice,
Promises kept, the strength,
Glorious victory.

Mary Hughes

WINTER SCAPEGOAT

A southern solstice
Spells trouble today for
Northern believers worshipping the sun

Cancelled garden party
Brings bias again for
Our fourth final season, which causes a change

Poor winter scapegoat
Blamed for their peculiar muddle
Winter scapegoat
Some do appreciate what you bring

Hopeful winter sun
Appearing over horizons
Sweeping winds upon wonderful weather
Long lonely winter scapegoat
Hated again for
Failure to learn to love always together

Sitting crystal snowflakes
Unmatched moments are none
Poor winter scapegoat
Don't worry
You shall be loved when you're gone.

Colin Jones

INDIAN SUMMER

Let's take a walk,
through alchemy and cold,
bronze, silver and gold.

September with its flame,
buzzing fruit and country lanes,
and rain on the side,
the green countryside.

The sun like an apple,
rosy in the trees,
October mists and autumnal looks,
and leaves and leaves and leaves.

Daylight and dew, the frost and you,
and let's tilt our heads upwards
to see with our eyes,
a holiday flight,
climbing high through candlelit skies.

M C Jones

SUMMER

Do you remember being young, with six long weeks off school?
And every day was sunny, warm and bright?
The weeks ahead stretched endlessly, with autumn far away,
And skies were blue, with not a cloud in sight.

Instead of bed by half-past eight, and fast asleep by nine,
(Which was the case if you had school next day)
You played outside while there was light, and weren't called in 'til ten,
And bedtime then was *still* an hour away!

A day down at the seaside with several of your friends
Was something you'd look forward to for days,
A good half hour on the bus past places rarely seen,
A whole new world would open to your gaze.

Once on the beach, unpack your lunch, but no surprises there,
The sandwich filling *always* was meat paste,
To drink an old 'pop' bottle filled with water from the tap,
No matter, you would see there was no waste.

A game of rounders, then a paddle, finish off your lunch,
By now the sandwich paste is mostly sand,
And passing round your water bottle (not a good idea!)
There's bits in there - it's *really* secondhand!

Back on the bus the journey home is mostly spent asleep,
The sun and salt-sea air have worked their spell.
An early night (no argument!), you're tired out by now,
Tomorrow's soon enough your tales to tell.

On other days, in different ways, the summer drifted by.
Then, suddenly, September's very near,
The nights are cooler, days grow shorter, garden fires slow burn.
Alas! The summer's gone until next year.

Geoffrey Leech

WINTER

Winter, brrrr, oh so cold,
Snowflakes all around.
Everywhere is white and bold,
Wonderful as if falls to the ground.

Children like to go and play,
Building snowmen large and small,
Throwing snowballs every day,
Pavements slippy, please don't fall.

The icy-cold wind starts to blow,
Makes your face start to glow,
Chills your body all over, inside,
Makes you rush home and want to hide.

Wintertime can be oh so dull,
Dark nights can be awful to some,
Yet others like the cold fresh air,
Some people don't really care.

S Longford

COLD COMFORT

Can't be doing with it,
All that rain and wind,
All that snow and fog,
When I'm out walking the dog.

Things freeze up,
The car won't start,
Anti-freeze needs topping.
To keep warm, on one foot I am hopping.

The weatherman fills my screen
With more of the same,
With isobars, showers, fronts and troughs.
Cant' go anywhere without our coats to doff.

The 'flu lays us low,
As it sweeps the country,
It's as if it's on a whistle-stop tour,
From town to town, calling at every door.

I must admit, a little snow is nice,
For Christmas, a few inches here and there,
Sets up the mood, goodwill to all and sundry,
As long as it falls on Friday and is gone again my Monday.

Now floods seem to be our main concern,
To follow the summer's drought,
We need bigger reservoirs to catch every drop and drip,
Adam's ale is so vital to us all, please don't gulp it down,
Just take a sip.

The black ice which took me to impact
With Mr Chalk's new garden wall,
Whoops, this wall had stood for only one week,
Now the bricks are broken and stacked in a heap.

So winter you can keep,
I won't lose any sleep.

P J Littlefield

STRIPPED

As the annual act reaches its climax
and the last leaves fall,
they stand stripped of their autumnal clothing;
unveiled,
exposing the beauty of their nakedness
to all those who turn to look.

Joy Morton

WINTER DEEP

Winter deep, winter asleep,
A bleak and silent season.
There seems no reason to leave
The comfort of the glowing fire.
A season sometimes set
In jewelled ice and snow,
When from the north,
A chill wind blows.
Lashing us with ice-crystal rain,
This thrashing; an ample reason to complain,
Though garment muffled from head to toes,
Behaving like lost and lonely Eskimos,
January and February blizzard time.
Summer sun now long forgotten,
To leave the house for a bit of fresh air,
Is deemed an odious crime.
The heating of the kitchen,
A warm meeting place,
Or greetings exchanged
By the welcoming open hearth,
Wood stacked, fire crackling,
Spitting, smoking and glowing red.
We laughing; a warm punch in hand.
Such a jolly gathering,
A very merry band,
Planning next season's garden.
The longed for summer holidays ahead,
Curtains drawn, air pleasantly warm,
Until we hasten to our comfy beds.

Julia Pegg

WINTER WONDERLAND

Old oak trees stand bolt upright underneath the weight -
Silent and strong they shed white tears
That are only visible when standing by their side.
A grown man crying can tilt the globe slightly a-kilter
And so it seems as if the snows have begun to fall again.

All around the country is like a frost ornamental shaker,
Trapped in this bubble of white mist, the breath of our maker.

A seething glow beyond is what's left of the sun
And even the German Shepherd crunches when he walks,
Being the only one that looks like a native
In this land of tossed and crumpled white blankets,
Where nothing moves save for the robins come to feast
On an ice-glossed table laden with crumbs -

For this is the land of the quick-fix and the blind eye
And it might happen there, but never to us.

The river below could host ice skaters if it freezes some more
But for now the rooftops bleed with melted snow.
Tonight, it is said, that the freeze will come again -
Tonight, with its ice torch and frantic legs desperately working,
Causing the pillowy powder to turn hard and don't you know that
                                        hard is treacherous -
Like parents who used to call a truce in the light of day
Only to resume the fight in the dark breath of night.

In chemistry they forget to tell you that sub-zero temperatures
Can also freeze time.

Shane O'Neill

WINTER POEM

Winter is here, winter is here,
It comes around this time of year.
You hear the jingles in the bells,
So many people as they yell.
The secret that's in all the magic,
Is never to fear, and never attack it.

Sheun Oshinbolu (11)

THOUGHTS ON AN OCTOBER EVE

The dying leaves take their final dance
As they are caught in a sudden wind.
They elegantly glide, swirl and whirl
As if indulging in a waltz by Strauss.
They flaunt their fleeting beauty
In exotic gowns of every hue,
Garbed in gold, green, ruby and ginger,
Burnished a burnt orange
By the now slowly setting sun.
Overhead the sky darkening to
A deep cobalt shade of blue,
The air growing ever colder,
As befits this evening in October.
Fallen leaves crunch underfoot,
Disintegrating, brittle already,
Returning to mould and dust
To exude the scent of fresh spices
From their kaleidoscopic beds.
The bleak cold of winter
Still a few weeks ahead,
My mind turns longingly to spring,
When once more life returns,
Flowers and leaves will once more
Take their turns to perform.
By then these leaves will have turned
To deep and sweet leaf mould.
I sigh for the sight of spring,
Turning, the trees in fading light still burning
Inspired, return to the warmth of my home fire.

Jonathan Pegg

AUTUMN CHANGES

Orangey blanket of ageing foliage,
rustling crackle of dried-up brunette leaves
lay amber-like, crinkled, turned upwards toward
amberish light of weak sun's rays that,
seep through bark arms and twiggy fingers.
Caught in a whirlpool of a blustery squall,
a winter garden quickly approaches,
a white enchantment to sneak upon us.
A rage is coming; its tempest is seen,
hibernation will soon begin.

Linda Pickering

UNTITLED

The green grass shone in the morning dew,
It was time to start the day anew.
The birds were singing with sheer delight
At the warmth of the sun
After the chill of night.
Nature's creatures glad to be alive,
The birds in their nest,
The bees in their hive.
All about them in hedgerow and field,
The crops to the sun, presenting their yield.
Seasons passed by, winter is near,
Cold winds now herald the coming new year.
The countryside is under snow,
Hibernating creatures are lying low.
Snug and cosy tucked up in their den,
They will not leave till the land warms again.
Nature casts its spell once more,
The April rain begins to pour.
The land once again comes alive,
The birds begin to sing,
The bees, they leave their hive,
Heralding the coming of spring.

Edward Hill

THE SLIDE

Young shoes slip back and forth, impatient
to corrupt the tiresome purity;
convert it to wicked black ice.

Instinctively all know the drill: the sprint,
the timely step as onto a fast-moving track.

Wind-wrapped, cheeks purpose-flushed puff steam,
arms lean on air, feet fly the path
of glass past squares of yellow panes
and shy high-steppers through an ermine-
muffled world.

Comes the sudden unwished end, where time
and again the tireless loop is held
intact; the fight against passivity
and fading light goes on.

An old man stops on trembling legs, smiles
ruefully down liver-spotted years.
His white-magic days defected to age,
the enemy; forcing him to walk wide.

All at once the game is up. Driven
by spite and right a crone with shovelled
ash emasculates the now ten metre-long
perfected sheen. Only the street lamp's
silver pool is left to shine.

Cries of injustice go unheard. Wet coats
are sullenly dragged on. They set off home
on heavy legs that with each step
grow lighter
at redeeming thoughts of tea.

Alan W Ruffles

ON A JANUARY MORNING
(For Beattie)

On a January morning
I opened my back door
to meet the shock of freezing air,
that slapped my face.
I stood back and gasped,
and everywhere was white.

It's a short walk to the bus stop.
Over the garden lay
a glittering white carpet,
untrodden and sparkling,
fragile and new.

Such peaceful landscape
so easily disturbed
by wellingtoned feet,
forming deep impressions
revealing an underlay
of dull, grey ice.

I trod with fervent respect,
taking care how to step
delicately, without falling
without hurting the snow,
making dimples in the icing
of a Christmas cake.

Jo S Reah

WINTER EXPLORERS

Grey dawn, windswept morn,
the wild geese fly high
long skeins across the cloud-hurrying sky.
We stand there, two young men alone,
and let our imaginations fly, want to explore -
go to where we have not been,
and perhaps may never get to go.
The winter world calls us to explore -
this is a lonely world and we hear and feel
nature's awakening, demanding call.
The snow, the ice, the wind,
the aurora at the Pole,
and we must answer for
we are young and know
we must follow, held as we are
in enduring winter's thrall.

Rick Storey

WINTER

The wind is icy cold,
There's frost upon the floor,
Your hands are dry and rough,
Your lips are chapped and sore.

You have to wrap up well
To keep the 'flu at bay,
And when the snow comes down,
The children like to play.

It's that time of year
To stay indoors and warm,
Keep the fires burning,
There might just be a storm.

Don't travel far from home,
Always staying near,
Snowstorms quickly come,
Now that winter's here.

L Sheppard

WONDERLAND LOST

Rising early I view the magic through my window
An eerie scene touched by fading moonglow

Snow-covered paths silently merge into the street beyond
Extending invisibly to the road, creating a picturesque bond.

The white world outside sleeps undisturbed,
No blade of grass, not even a footprint is observed

The scene is breathtaking, like a picture frozen in time
I brush my hand across the windowpane, the outline to define.

Wait! Here comes the paper boy daring to spoil the scene
He drags his feet and kicks the snow disrupting where he's been.

The milkman follows soon after and leaves ridges in the snow
My picture becomes ruined as he trudges to and fro.

Now appears the postman slamming gates, rattling doors
My white world yields to the activities of these many chores.

Wonderland lost!

Dawn Sansum

THE MOON ON THE SLIDE

It took me ages to perfect it I remember.
All that tamping down and careful smoothing,
Getting every inch just right.
I remember as if it was yesterday,
Rushing back outside after tea
Into the freezing night air.
Rustling past the frosted privets,
Running out onto the street.
I'd never seen diamonds.
Here was magic that shone like mounds of glitter
Poured onto my world from a fairy's hand.
I got to work, slipping and sliding,
Patting and smoothing the illuminated snow.
Rubbing and polishing, rubbing and polishing,
Till at last it was ready to try . . .
Four strong running steps, then
Whoosh!
Flying on the icy run!
Night air rushing past my ears,
Then with flailing limbs, grabbing the lamp post,
Gloves still wet from morning's snowballing and
Collapsing in stifled giggles,
Brushing strands of wet hair from my mouth.
Yes, those childhood delights remain with me even now,
The enchantment of fairy glitter and
The moon on the slide.

Anna Shannon

THE SUMMER ROSE

The bush that was in summer crowned
With lovely roses, stands bare, its beauty gone.
Beneath, unheaded on the ground
Lie the petals that have fallen one by one.

The tree that gave us shade from the noonday sun
Uplifts bare arms against a cloudier sky
Wind-stripped - all its leaves are gone
Autumn's here - and winter's nigh.

Soon will come the evening chills
The valleys fill with rolling mists
White edges trim the nearby hills
All in the grasp of Jack Frost's fists.

Another year is drawing to its close,
Ere soon its journey will be run
Keep fresh the memory of that lovely rose
Hope next year, you'll get a better one.

H H Steventon

WHEN HERE

As summer closes
The door to autumn opens.
Goodbye to the swift
And swallow.
May your journey
Start with song.
Farewell to the martins,
Your nests and hollows.
The time has come
To release and bless.

Heads of summer flowers,
Now faded,
Open to the winds
Where seeds like capsules
Spring forth
With distant life
Instilled.

The season gathers speed.
And nights
Close the doors
To youth and playfulness.
Gone the idle wanderings
Of mind and heart
And sun's relaxing touch.
For soon the death
Of all that's passed.
And cleansing snow
Shall wipe all tears
Away.

Lyn Sandford

SPRING

Herald spring trumpets yellow daffodils
He dresses the land with fresh green leaves.
From his cloak, he scatters birds, bees and butterflies
With watchful blue sky-eyes, he marches on,
Towards April and May, Twin sisters of spring.

Kenneth I Squires

SNOWBALL FIGHT

Snow;
Fresh fallen
As the evening light
Faded into shadows of the deepening night,
Cold to the touch, soft and light,
Delicate, fragile almost,
Beautiful, if undisturbed.
But, we were young,
Our youth would not be curbed
And heedless of the need for quiet
We romped, we weaved,
We searched each other out,
Scored hit after hit
With those soft mounds of joy,
Our laughter muffled by our play.

Strangers we had been, just the other day,
And this a lonely, dreadful place.
Friends now
And something of our private ecstasy
Was evident, I do believe,
When,
Soaked, red from exertion,
Chilled to the bone but quite relaxed
We bade each other quiet, 'Goodnight'
And, just as quietly,
Went to bed.

D J Totten

THE GOLDEN SEASONS

As all the leaves on the trees
Turn gold, silver and brown
And all the birds fly south
For the winter,
I slowly walk through
Those silent woods
And remember the good and happy times
When I walked hand in hand
Along the golden sands
With an angel from Heaven above.
With an angel of beauty
I will always love
With the whole of my heart and soul
And whose sweet angel name was Wendy Baron.

But that was long ago,
When I was young and free,
And now that the seasons are changing,
No longer is she with me,
But I will always remember the seasons,
The golden seasons that she walked by my side
As my warm and tender, loving bride.

Donald John Tye

APPOINTED TO SPRING

O profound love,
that exceeds day to day -

I am appointed to spring
and her supple charms of endearment.
Like the holly on the tree in winter,
or the festive yew,
I am in that garden of words.
I am taxed to this vocation
and digest love so sweetly.

And all love flourishes
from a learned heart -
to forces wave of eager understanding
into spring's own delight
of mirrored attraction.

That takes to summer and winter
all into one -
four seasons of restful thinking
a home-made harvest of replenishment.

All for a Saviour's love
and given embrace
of human modesty
and faced reality
till the cows come home
over the vale after milking
and in silent slumbers we sleep.

Roger Thornton

RED, YELLOW

No Fauve could have bettered it.
A spry scarlet oak sapling
lorded its emerald site
with red, red spotlights coupling
with the silence and the heat
to make October startle
my eyes with its sanguine heart.

And a tulip tree, its head
a deep impressionist sky
brushed like a belly of cloud
yellowed, yellowed the late day.
Briefly past and future fled -
only a quintessential
bottomless breath was abroad.

Chris White

SPRING STORM

Soft the primroses!
Subtly sweet!
Brushed by breezes!
Sweeping my feet.
Green valleys!
Rolling beyond!
As rainbows form
From the clouds to the land.
Purples, pinks,
Deepen, then fade,
Often I think . . .
How are they made?
My heart rejoices,
The sights, sounds,
Red-breasted robins
Go bobbing around.

Dandelion clocks,
Flutter, then sway!
Buttercups brighten
A springtime in May!
Blossoms, brackens,
Trees overhung,
This way, that way,
Kissed by the sun!
Delicately formed!
Feathery light!
Torn by the storm
That battered the night.

Wendy Watkin

FIRST OF MORNING

Frosty glistening coated
Encrusted scenes abound
Everywhere deep chilled
While nature's dawn chorus
Utters ne'er a sound.

Nothing stirs
Incapable of movement
Stuck - earthly bound
Frost's vice-like grip
Holds all - compound

Yet still 'needs must'
As we venture forward
First of morning - pound
Why all else
Is frost-encrusted found.

Gary J Finlay

WINTER

Makes me dislike early morning
Keeps me yawning
Makes me hate outdoors
Because of the wet floor
Winter winds hate my organs
No protection even in a coat from Morgan's
Uh, there goes my ear
I wish I had the furs of a polar bear
I can't feel my fingers
I can't hear the singers
Oh, that's got nothing to do with winter
Someone quick, put on the heater,
Oh yeah, no heater outside
I need to get my behind inside
I think my brain cells are frozen
Because I think my fingers are a dozen
There goes the beautiful snowflakes
Slippery . . . it can make your bones break
Winter has so many disadvantages
I can't, so can anyone think of advantages?

Ify Helen Nzegwu

SPRINGTIME

A blackbird sings along to the dawn chorus.
The daffodils are dancing in the soft breeze.
Newborn lambs romp, in a lush green field.
And pink blossom adorns the trees.

Deer are running free in the forest
Primroses snuggle into the hedgerow.
Baby birds peer out of their nests
And now we've seen the last of the snow.

The beautiful smell from the freesias,
A carpet of bluebells stretched out on the floor.
The tranquil sound of a babbling brook
For spring is upon us once more.

J Drury

JACK FROST

Jack Frost has crept stealthily in overnight,
Covering the landscape in a blanket of white,
In sparkling patterns that are such a delight,
His fingers have etched pictures that change with the light.
Oh the dark side, however, there is danger out of sight,
Once in its grip you're in a bit of a plight.
It's a case of fingers crossed and hold on tight!
But on a cheerful note, the sudden chill kills off germs that are
at their height

A touch of frost and they'll soon take flight.
The clear sky Jack has brought with him soon makes everything
look bright,

It will transform the day; you'll be full of delight.

Margaret Blight

SEASONS' BEAUTY (IT'S SO LOVELY)

I love a clear night with the
Moon shining so bright.
Light from distant stars
That give wondrous light.

I love spring with golden daffodils
I did love wild daffodils
That grew in all fields
I love spring's pretty flowers
I love to take a sketchbook and
Draw for hours and hours.

I love Maytime blossoms
All so divine.
I love summer, with its heat
I even love hot nights
Humid when you fail to sleep.
I love many summer flowers
Here again I sketch for hours and hours.

Best of all I love autumn,
Red, gold and brown.
I love falling leaves
Golden beech shining through the rain
I still love all this
Filling the gutters again.

I love winter, white virgin snow
Cannot start the car, thank God
We will not have to go!
I really, really love Christmas lights
Presents, singing to the Lord.
All things we have bought we love
But cannot afford.
I love white frost on rock hard ground
Such crunching sound.

Nature's response
Discovers such captivating beauty
Some to fade as Earth's seasons pass
Many ways and days.

Pamela Hopes

SNOW

Nature's wonderful creation
Gently falling from the sky
Individual and special in every way
The simple snowflake arrives
So delicate and a pure delight
A sign that winter is here
Settling undisturbed such a pleasing sight
Covering the earth before our very eyes
Admiration can quickly turn to horror
Swirling snowstorms bringing devastation
The dense blanket formed, freezing the earth
A death sentence to fauna and flora alike
The idyllic picture sadly no more
Hypothermia is now a threat
Do not despair as the climate warms
The snow melts away and causes no more harm
Winter's picture rapidly disappears
Snow is best depicted on the Christmas cards.

Anne Sackey

HOLLY BRIGHTENS JANUARY

That would be the grimmest
Month, if it weren't for holly
Leaves being polished, as they come
From buds. Berries succumb
To bills of birds, needful optimists.

Through December's poor eye
Wildlife looks at winter;
While red beads bejewel
Hedges, we know that cruel
Season soon will pass by.

Gillian Fisher

NOT SO BAD

I dread the arrival of winter and indoors confined,
Find that the dark, depressing days play havoc with my mind.
A feeling of doom pervades my very soul, takes over,
Hate winter mornings peeping over the duvet cover.

Because all I see then is blackness staring back at me,
Drift back to sleep, thinking of places I would rather be.
Eventually rise, greet the cold dampness of the day,
Christmas, is only hope on the horizon I must say.

I really would like to give this sombre season a miss,
If I did, would have to forego husband's mistletoe kiss.
On reflection, not that bad encased in the warmth inside,
If weather's not atrocious can drive out to countryside.

S Mullinger

WINTER

Winter is a season, so it seems,
Of crazy happenings, given to extremes.
Early winter brings storms and violent weather,
Wild winds, high tides, fierce rain - and all together!
Riverside dwellers suffer the inundating flood,
And damage from that awful, stinking mud.
Then, just when discouraged, we feel tired and weary,
(And that winter days are always dull and dreary),
Comes Guy Fawkes night and firework displays,
And children's fun to brighten up our days.
While bonfires help us to 'remember',
Fog slows the traffic, and reminds us it's November.

Then comes Christmas, with its wondrous story
Of the manger-baby, angels in their glory,
Shepherds, wise men, presents! Christmas cheer
Dispels depression - makes it disappear.

January's high winds hit buildings, blow down trees.
Soon, then, the elements may settle to a lengthy freeze.
Deep snow may fall. It comes like a thief in the night
To transform the world into robes of dazzling white.
At first, ice-pictures and snow scenes will delight us,
And snowmen, skating, sliding, skiing, can excite us.
But those who drive, or work outside, know it will mean
Harsh conditions - so they are not so keen!
Soon it will thaw and slowly - we must hope,
For those fearing floods again, that they can cope.
So winter, a crazy mixed-up season, ekes out its hours,
And April brings some sunshine - and spring showers!

Robert T Collins

WINTER

Grey and overcast, the morn
Stating clearly, summer's gone.
Heavily the prospect weighs,
Long dark nights, dreary days.
Forecasts piling woe on woe.
Rain and hail, sleet and snow,
Rough winds pound and roar
Monotonously round the door.
Small wonder folk relocate,
As for me - I'll hibernate.

Sue Cann

BEING OLD IN WINTER!

I'm shivering, shivering, it's cold in my home,
I'm old and frail, and live on my own,
I gaze out the window at the sky dull and grey,
I've looked at the forecast, it will snow later today.

The snow is now falling, it's getting quite thick,
If we get a hard frost, I'm sure it will stick,
Icicles hang menacing from the window frame,
A robin on the window sill, it really is so tame.

I'm going for a blanket, I really feel the cold,
I think my blood must be thin, it's part of being old,
Children in next door's garden, build a snowman for their mum,
It's the time that kids love, when they can have some fun.

I really hate the winter, having to stay indoors,
Listening to the tick of the clock and gazing at wooden floors,
I long to hear the birds sing, and daffs begin to grow,
And have the sun's warmth on my bones and an ending to the snow.

I E Percival

WINTER IS HERE!

Raw, cold mornings, ice patches on ground,
snow-muffled streets, so barely a sound.
Trees black-etched, bereft of leaves,
bent by strong wind as it weaves
soughing through the branches bare,
for once more - winter is here!
It hurls the snow against the pane,
a pause, and then it strikes again.

Shrubs festooned in virgin white
form a really lovely sight.
Nature with her magic hand
creates a perfect wonderland.
Cobwebs silvered by the frost -
spider - moribund - home has lost.
Icicles so long and straight
hang beside the garden gate.

Snowmen spring up everywhere
carrot nose and piercing stare.
Snowballs fly as battles rage -
often the distance hard to gauge,
and crash against the windowpanes -
broken glass on pathway rains!
We freeze as we await the train
to find it's cancelled once again!

Children outside all day will play
and rush downhill on home-made sleigh,
or thrill to walk on pristine snow
leaving footprints as they go.
But, sadly, it will turn to slush
and travel to gutter in hectic rush -
then cleared away by heavy rain
to join the flood in heaving drain.

Chilblain-misery on our toes,
bright red cheeks, and brighter nose!
The nights are long, and dark and cold;
hunger makes the birds so bold
they come right up to door or sill
begging for crumbs, and take their fill.
The nights draw in, the day has gone -
by 4 o'clock the lights are on.

As pale, cold moon comes into sight
blinds are drawn against the night.
We spare a thought for those outside
freezing in this wintertide.
We settle by a cosy fire
dressed in all manner of attire!
And dream of summer when we'll be
cooling off beside the sea!

Joyce Hockley

WINTER

Snow on roof and snow on tree,
On field and fen, on you and me.
See the soft flakes flutter down,
Covering country, covering town.
Winter comes and by surprise
The world is changed before our eyes.
What was black and bleak and bare
Becomes a palace standing there.
Lakes are frozen, mirrored scenes
Pure and white, as in our dreams.
Towns no longer drab and grey
But mantled in snow along the way.
Filigree snowflakes falling down,
Enough to make an angel's crown.
Our garden now no longer drear
For England's wintertime is here!

Peggy Briston

WINTER PRELUDE

As summer passes on her way
a freshness fills the air.
The swallow and the martin
will be flying off somewhere.
As I take the woodland path
there is a rustle in the trees.
I can hear a whispering
of the last summer breeze.
Nature's clock is ticking,
it is time to change her frock.
From emerald green to golden
brown. Tick-tock, tick-tock, tick-tock.
Too soon the leaves are falling,
squirrels rushing everywhere.
Gathering every nut they find
and storing it with care.
Yet the little robin sings
for he is quite content,
for grubs are in abundance
a feast that's heaven sent.
Robin make the most of plenty
for autumn will not last.
Too soon autumn will be gone,
you will feel the winter's blast.

Irene Keeling

WINTER

The Christmas card shows an inviting scene
Of crisp white snow and bright red berries,
A wonderland, a land of might-have-been,
With children, scarved, their faces red as cherries.
A country cottage, its chimney leaking smoke,
Reminder of the glowing fire inside,
Whilst evergreens, and Christmas lights evoke
An eager, joyous, wondrous, mad sleigh ride.
Well-being fills the air with tidings of good cheer,
And carollers their message loud forth tell
The season of goodwill and hope is surely here,
And all the signs and portents augur well.
But is it really so? Just face the actual facts,
And feel the biting, creeping, raw, insidious cold
Which stealthily moves in, and soon impacts,
And with its icy, vice-like grip takes hold.
Grey skies and brooding clouds the senses drain,
As coughs and sneezes rasp the wintry air,
And crisp white snow soon turns to slush in chilling rain
To mingle with the grimy earth in sad despair.
The outside pipes begin to freeze and leak,
With plumbers, like the sun, in short supply,
Draughts stalk the windy corners playing hide-and-seek,
All nature seems to falter, slowly die.
So winter has two sides, the dark and bright,
And inner warmth and outer cold their varied pleasures bring,
Each mood, each picture brings its own delight
To take us on, at last, to the renewing spring.

Jack Scrafton

THE AUTUMN OF MY LIFE

Autumn - is happening to me
yes me!
Is my summer nearly past
I wonder?
The blossoms that have fallen
won't revive.
Some of the light has gone
from my eye.
Will I weather the coming winter
so well?
The spring weather always comes,
but I find
that my agility is lessened.
Buds burst,
lovely flowers, blossom effortlessly,
yet I
don't seem to have their energies.
oh dear,
has life passed me by? No!
As limbs tire
I look to Jesus for strength.
And pray
for renewed mind and spirit,
and ask
what can I do for Him now?
Our lives can
have seasons of autumn fruitfulness.

Beryl Lenihan

OVERTURE TO AUTUMN

Impatiently, autumn waits in the wings,
While summer still has centre stage
As the sun filters its glorious rays
Through trees green and full-blown.
Mid-September past and the squirrels delight
In their almost frantic search for acorns
Under the enormous spreading oak
Which has given sequestered shade
For many decades in this mid-city park.
Office workers, baring arms and legs,
Sit on benches or the dry, sparse grass,
Determined to soak up as much sun
As their dinner hour will allow.
Pigeons coo contentedly, bobbing from side to side,
Claws scrunching on fallen beech mast,
To pick up sandwich scraps, then glide 'en masse'
'Neath leafy, lowering branches to find
A more encouraging, nourishing spot.
Flowers still flaunt their jewelled blooms
In well-tended, rail-encircled beds.
This past growing season long, warm and sunny.
Puffed-out roses cling to their delicate parchment petals
As if eager to please for as long as they can.
The set is serene, bathed in contentment
For man, fauna and flora.

What a difference a month or two will make!
Trees shivering their shrivelled leaves to the soil.
Gnarled limbs pleading to a doleful sky,
People hurrying through the park
Limbs cosseted under warm layers,
No thought of lazy lingering,
Even the squirrels scurrying about their business.
Now unhindered by dense foliage,
They'll trapeze from bare branch to twig tips,
Summer exhaustion culminating in cosy hibernation.

Even the birds will disappear, gone
In the absence of nuts and picnic scraps.
The park will relax when Autumn prompts Winter's cue.
On it will come, a restful part, few spectators,
Except the wind, rain, frost and snow
To add to the trees' weathered scars.
But, deep down in the icy soil, miracles will be afoot!
Hundreds of daffodil bulbs will be swelling
To soon thrust forth their golden splendour
To warm the hearts of winter-weary workers
Who traverse the park from home to office and back again.

Pat Heppel

SEPTEMBER

In early morn ethereal mists
    Drift over fairy lands,
And pearls of dew deck cobweb lace
    In many sparkling strands

Which stretch from bush to bush
    In September's hazy dawns,
Then vanish as the sun breaks through
    And dries the spangled lawns.

September days are not so long
    But their warmth is clear and fresh.
The new turned earth throws up its scent,
    It lingers on our breath.

The hedgerows now along the lanes
    Are hung with jewels bright
Gleaming in September sun,
    A feast of sheer delight.

Blue fruit of sloe and elder,
    Crab apples gnarled but sweet,
Blackberries clustered rich and dark -
    A luscious tempting treat.

Hawthorns are hung with crimson fruit
    And rose hips' scarlet glow.
The chestnut drops its conkers brown
    For questing boys below.

Beneath the oaks the acorns lie
    Ripe brown in their small green cups,
And the droning bee, still busy,
    From late honeysuckle sups.

The hazelnuts are also ripe,
    And teazles full of seed
Provide the small bright goldcrest
    With a satisfying feed.

The seeds of the grasses abundantly
    Are scattered all around
As September's horn of plenty
    Is spread across the ground.

In fields at dawn the mushrooms
    Push through the dark rich soil
And nestle in the dew-damp grass,
    A veritable spoil

Of treasure for the gatherer
    Who cares to search and find
The bounty which September
    Provides of every kind.

Frances Marie Cecelia Harvey

SUMMER SOUNDS

Oh the magic of those summer sounds
the lazy baying of reluctant hounds
the gentle twittering of birds
and lowing of the meadow herds

The pigeon cooing to his mate
the creaking of that rustic gate
the frantic buzzing of the bees
and soft breeze rustling through the trees

The pitter-pat of gentle rain
and wild geese honking in the lane
piglets grunting in their sty
and roar of thunder in the sky

At times we hear a young lamb cry
or sound of horses galloping by
the call of coot or duck on lake
the cockerel telling us to wake

The hooting of a far-off train
the droning of an aeroplane
a gardener whistling cheerfully
and lapping waves in deep blue sea.

Young fox cubs who play and scream
the tinkling of that silver stream
the badgers' noisy barks at night
the hoot of owl that gives a fright!

How lucky to have sight and sound
of nature's beauty all around
we thank our Lord in Heaven above
for gifts He gives with so much love.

Pat Rogers

SUMMER FUN

Bramble thorns and nettle stings
The mosquito delights with buzzing wings
Peeling skin and baking sun
Is all part of summer fun

Moaning children, far too hot
Trying to find shady spot
Waste bins flow with all that's best
The constant joy of a wasp's nest

The wind blows sand along the ground
Swirling dust clouds all around
Turning skin into emery boards
Invading all like Mongol hordes.

Days too long, the sun's too bright
Too hot to sleep every night
Autumn waits for her turn to reign
To save us all from summer pain.

Bill Peters

SUMMER

Sunshine and brightness,
Swimsuits and t-shirts, brill'nt in whiteness,
A nonchalant saunter
By fast flowing water,
Sun tan and lotion,
A dip in the ocean,
Deckchairs and ices,
Holiday surprises.
Hiking and biking,
Rowing and towing,
Coming and going
On road, rail and airway
Rushing to get away . . .

Swallows are nesting,
Teachers are resting,
Roses are blooming,
Honey bees humming,
Baby birds flying,
Spring flow'rs dying,
Wheat fields a-swaying,
And lovers delaying
Saying 'goodnight'
. . . At the gate, they wait,
And forget time until late.

Summer fruits growing,
Farmers are knowing
Harvest's a-plenty,
The barns won't be empty.
The harsh winds are calmer,
The evenings warmer,
Perfume and colour
Greet the newcomer
And spread the delight of glorious summer.

Jean Duckworth

THE FALL

Autumn's chill is in the air,
Its hazy presence everywhere.
Days grow short and nights are long
And birds are sparing with their song.

Trees rejoice and proudly hold
Aloft their leaves of burnished gold.
The wind awaits with pent-up sound
To send them tumbling to the ground.

The shadows lengthen, sun is low,
As swifts and swallows homeward go.
Ploughs and harvesters are stilled
And barns with new-mown hay are filled.

The ripened fruits are gathered in,
Firm and full and smooth of skin.
All around church bells are rung
And hymns of harvest home are sung.

Frank Jensen

AUTUMN SUNSET

You stand there framed in autumn's sunset,
Big white sails stilled, you the sentinel of the fen.
Your reflection in the lake the picture set.
Quiet and still, no more work for mill and men.
Will you stand serene to watch and wait,
Till next year's harvest comes thro' mill gate.

This picture will in my memory stay,
For you are my past that has been forgot.
Strong in heart you have stood by.
Let's hope your days are not.
Refurbished are some, others left to rot?
Those with new life will restore me to yesterday.

Let me stand here to see this majesty
To try and imagine what life used to be,
When autumn sun shone through your sails,
And miller's wife would hear gossip's tales.
Would'st not we all should have this memory
Of nature's wonders and its tranquillity.

Softly autumn sun shines on this fable
To paint this scene, as would Constable.
Then hang this picture in my mind
For when would I such beauty find.
Through all seasons beauty will come,
But for me, my love is autumn.

John Clarke

Mother In Autumn

It is autumn now,
the nearness of the end of years,
the time of failing zeniths
and the growing cold days.

A remembered summer stays
bright with season's colours,
burning in the mind and leaves
before they fall.

But this is the first of all
my years of visiting
she has not wished to travel out
and revel in this fine defiance
as the winter nears.
It is autumn now,
the approach of end of years.

Ray Dunn

LATE SEPTEMBER

Late September day breaks cool with mist
Winds catch the leaves as they turn and twist.
Mornings lose their light and as the day closes
Savour the fragrance of the last of the roses.
Everywhere looks cooler, crisper
Squirrels start hoarding they've heard the whisper.
Damp grasses wet under foot,
Birds eating last berries and nut.
Trees with colour fading fast
Bright skies too bright to last.
Butterflies go with frosty night,
Swallows preen then circle ready for flight.
Summer flowers lose their splendour,
It's a seasonal thing late September.

Vera Collins

AUTUMN

I love the autumn season it fills me with awe,
Tried to describe my feelings many times before,
Poets through the ages, more learned than I
Captured so expressively
Wonderful pictures for us to see.

Keats once gazed with delight
At each picturesque sight,
Trees dressed in multicoloured gowns,
Leaves in wonderful shades
Of orange-gold, russet browns.

Fruit hangs heavy on solid branches
Field hands come to pick the crop,
Climbing high, they fill the baskets
Reach the best fruit at the top.

This wonderful season; autumn.

Lil Bordessa

SOME THOUGHTS ON AUTUMN'S ARRIVAL

Would you believe another summer's fled?
Those leaves which yesterday greened tree and bush
With rich warm shades of russet, gold and red
The autumn's artist splashes with his brush.

We pause, and wonder where the year has gone
Since we sang our joy that first day of spring;
We pause again to ponder, now and anon,
What winter and the coming year may bring.

But whether we look back across the year,
Or try to see into the one to come,
There is a certainty to give us cheer
No matter where our wayward thoughts may roam;

After winter's cold snow and chilling rain
Spring will return and warm us once again!

Dan Pugh

THE FALL

Flutter down October leaves
It's time you parted from the trees
We await your blanket on the ground
Of russet, gold and chestnut brown
Eager to feel beneath our feet
Your crisp and crunchy autumn treat.

Sharon Brewer

AUTUMN TREASURE

Autumn is a treasure trove for all to behold,
Every tree that you see is a different shade of gold.
Not treasure in the sense of value you see,
But there's tons and tons of it, and it's absolutely free.

You can't lodge it in a bank or a safety box
You can gather it in armfuls yet it doesn't need locks
You can put it on the compost heap to make leaf mould,
In spring next year it will be worth its weight in gold.

And so this autumn treasure I am sure you will agree
Is beautiful, and as said before, is absolutely free.
Take advantage of it being there, for it's not long to stay,
Make the most of nature's bounty ere' the winds blow it away.

Helen Lock

AUTUMN

Long summer days and long summer nights
Are now just memories, out of our sights;
The days are shortening as winter draws near,
Now that the season of autumn is here.

Grey skies above us, thickening clouds;
Where are you summer? Where are your crowds?
Of holidaymakers packed on the beach,
Now the bleak shoreline seems out of reach.

Strong October gales, bring the trees down,
Whip up the sea, so people might drown;
Ships blown adrift for hour after hour,
This when autumn really turns sour.

But autumn can have her good side too,
Trees wear new dresses of every hue;
Reds, golds and browns of many a shade,
Such autumn glory is not man-made.

Trees sing their praises to God on high,
As they rustle their leaves to the sky;
Strong autumn breezes blow the leaves down,
Now a carpet, instead of a crown.

Irene Hart

CIRCLE OF LIFE

As the light changes and the air becomes crisp
When the sun hangs low in the sky and the days are shorter
Geese, like trailing strands of ribbons fly past on practice flights
Picking up stragglers, losing the weak
Calling to one another with claxton voices
A sound to alert those below of their passage
We rush from our homes to say our farewells
As we watch six V-shaped squadrons fly over the land
God bless, good luck, safe journey, we mentally shout
See you next year, next year, next year.

Susan Lewis

AUTUMN THOUGHTS

Burnished golds of autumn leaves,
laced with a vibrant cocktail
of ripening fruits, full of nourishment,
to sustain through weary winter
grace the hedgerows and forests;
where bare branches, dusted
with frozen cobwebs, will shiver
and sleep before the gentle rebirth

of spring . . .

Anita Richards

SUMMER SUNDAY

Looking up to the blue, blue sky
Looking up as a tiny bird flies by.
Cotton wool floats by me.
Not surgical swabs,
But fluffy seeds of life searching
For somewhere to settle.
Life can be so cold and surgical,
Yet, the sun warms us freely,
The birds sing,
The breeze warms our cool bodies.
                              Serenity exists

The breeze whispers through the grass.
The poplars sway enticingly.
                              More thoughts . . .
Four graceful herons span the tree tops,
A tiny butterfly settles on my leg.
A spider on my t-shirt walks over the letter 'A'
In Age Concern!
Tiny harmless creature, I share your space . . .
I lay in a disused churchyard, yet life surrounds me.
No morbidity here.
Leaves may fall, spent and withered,
But roses bloom . . .
Someone somewhere plays life's tune.

Moving.
Back to reality, the butterfly gone . . .
I place the tiny spider on the leaf of a tree.
Yes, life goes on . . .

Liz Osmond

Morning Glory

Cold, bright, brilliant light,
Silver frost settled unbroken.
The pond solid with packed ice.
Moorhens skating, looking for thaw.
Fish unseen under the solid covering
Breath opaque as it touches the air.
Ghost-like branches pure against the winter sun,
Icicles hang heavy with their burden.
The stillness of the morning
Uninterrupted
Bird-like patterns unbroken by pressure.
Everything carries calmness and tranquillity.
Relish the moment
It will pass
And the warmth of the day will break the spell.

Gael Nash

AUTUMN THOUGHTS

Autumn's riches are soon spent
On pavements wet with salty tears.
Kind sun sends down some winter warmth
To fill my heart with blithe good cheer.
Russet carpets underfoot
Muffle my tread as on I go
Strolling along in pensive mood
Sighing at thoughts of drifting snow.
All seasons change, time marches on.
Spring turns to summer
Nothing lasts
But summer one day will return
To banish thoughts of winter's blasts.

Rosemary Thomson

SPRINGTIME

Spring brings new beginnings
To everything on earth,
A wondrous sight to be seen
Everywhere rebirth.

Trees and flowers gradually
Open to the world,
A mass of colours on display
Their beauty they unfurled.

Creatures of every size
Send out their mating call,
No time to waste, spring has arrived
A busy time for all.

Rainbow appears in cloudy sky
Soft showers soon will bring,
Tiny plants from soft brown earth
Greeting the birth of spring.

Birds, bees, flowers and trees
Every living thing,
Waking from winter's grip
Welcoming the spring.

J Naylor

BARE

Denuded trees
Stand all around
Vulnerable
Bare
Their branches
Stretch out to
Embrace the chill
Autumnal air
While on the ground
Is spread
A crisp carpet
Of wondrous hue.

Geraldine Laker

AUTUMN

As the temperatures nudge into the 100's
On these long hot August days
It's hard to imagine that in a month or so
We'll be entering a different phase

When the nights will at last be cooler
As we watch the autumn appear
The leaves will change from green to gold
At that glorious time of year

We can walk in the park or the countryside
As life slows to a gentler pace
When Mother Nature shows her full maturity
In the beauty of autumn's face.

Barbara Manning

THE CONKER NECKLACE

Every year when autumn comes around
And conkers that shine like jewels, fall to the ground
Fond memories of my mother I recall
Of happy bygone days when I was small

We used to go collecting conkers with a smile on our face
Taking them home to make a fine conker necklace
Together we would thread them on golden twine
Making a necklace of perfection and it was mine.

Those happy bygone days are ever in my mind
Even now on autumn days if a conker I find
I pick up the shining brown jewel, my precious stone
And fond memories return, but now I walk alone.

Once again the beautiful conker necklace I recall
And walking in autumn sunshine, with my mother when I was small,
Seeing the leaves of red and gold drift slowly down to rest
Treasured memories of autumn linger, the season I like best.

Brenda Casburn Colvin

THE WAITING EARTH

Red, brown, bronze and golden leaves cascading to the ground,
floating lightly on the breeze, softly carpeting
the woodland soil, they do not make a sound.
The chill, cool winds of autumn, a misty morning sun,
the long warm lazy days of summer, now are gone and done.
Children gather around the bonfires,
smoke drifting lazily to the gloomy sky,
birds are circling all around, to warmer lands far away,
they are soon to fly.
Marmalades, jams and pickles,
stored on the shelves, all lined up in a row
the farmer working hard now,
gathering in the last of the earth's good crop before the winter's snow.
So, silently we all wait now,
to hear the proclamation of the boy child's wondrous birth,
a pale cold moon up in the sky,
shines upon the waiting earth.

Dorothy Chadwick

EARLY AUTUMN

Fir trees tower over Tamerisk
whose gossamer green boughs bow down
to greet cream flowers of clover
in this mid August clime.

The laburnum so golden in May time
has succumbed to the autumn sun
where once golden chains glistened
only crisp brown ringlets remain.

Over the way, corn field stubble is golden
where birds search for insects and then
in unison fly over to the woodland to roost
until the dew rises again.

Blackberries are ripe for picking
upon the hedgerows steep and here
in West Sussex each season is
especially special for me.

While the corn stacks await farm truck loader
behind a ridge of oak trees then soon this
August harvest will be gathered in.

The bells from the church on the hill-top
ring out across meadow and plain for this
the glory of countryside
a round up of memories reclaimed.

Hazel Sheppard

Autumn

It's still mild enough
To spend a few hours on the beach,
To enjoy the warmth of the gentle mid afternoon sun.
Pullovers and cardigans, maybe even jackets, are in order now,
The time for sunbathing in swimming costumes and shorts
Is long past.
But time enough
To watch the children and young people play,
Time enough to remember the strong heat of high summer
And hope to see another.

B W Ford

THE HUSH OF AN AUTUMN EVENING

When the sun begins to slide down the sky
and the playful breeze becomes tired,
the trees cease to resist and change
their conversation to a whisper.
The lights begin to shimmer afar off
and the first star appears in the velvet blue.
Flowers close and birds call their 'goodnights'
as a coolness creeps over the land.
Dark shadows deepen everywhere
and the hush of all noiselessness
becomes the loudest sound.
Then do we know the peace of God
when we become receptive
to the sound of silence.

Mena H A Faulkner

FINALLY

As the bright leaves of autumn fall and fade
I watch your life ebbing slowly away.
I see hope die in my mother's eyes
And I cannot comfort her.

Doctors sit beside your bed to say
In well-meant ambiguity
That death is insistent,
The battle is lost.

I have loved you all my life;
I don't know how to let you go;
But, as darkness covers the drifting leaves,
I know finally that I cannot keep you.

Valerie Sutton

AUTUMN

The swallows are gathering for their annual flight
Seeking out warmer climes.
But how do they know when the time is right
And how do they follow the signs?
As if by a magic calendar
On which they recorded the date
The cables are lined by hundreds of birds
United by the time to migrate.
So, adieu little ones
And from you may we learn
To be patient as winter goes by,
And be happy to know
As we watch you go -
Next summer you'll surely return.

D Harvey

AUTUMN

Drizzle slides down the windows
as damp trickles into houses and bones.
Brown patches of grass gladden to green again.
Leaves flaunt their verdant variety,
defying encroaching winter
which will leach their colours
and loose them from their anchorage.
Late roses bloom valiantly
amid glowing chrysanthemums.
Birds vee their southward flight
and wasps and bees swoop sleepily
in the cooling days. The light itself
mellows and diminishes
as the earth settles down to sleep.

Marion Porter

AUTUMN

With a smell of rich crumbling
trees disperse their hoarded summer,
fling unhesitating every
last leaf down, retaining nothing.
Ready once more to display their
nakedness, with all the beauty
of their weathered bones.

Idris Woodfield

AUTUMN THOUGHT

A utumn is a time for reflection,
U nderstanding that life is a journey
T omorrow may bring joy or maybe sorrow,
U nless we learn from the past we only
M ake the same mistakes over and over again.
N ow let's endeavour to build a better world for future generations.

T oo many possessions can lead to misery,
H ow we need to learn to share with others.
O penness is the key to good relationships,
U nkept promises cause destruction,
G lobal warming has brought floods,
H onour your marriage vows,
T rust in God.

Cathy Mearman

LATE AUTUMN

The trees clung to their leaves
well into November that autumn,
defying nature in warmer weather,
turning increasingly violent shades
of russet and crimson,
burning to keep their gold.
The storms forgot them,
the wind simply failed to turn up,
so they wore their shrivelled mourning clothes
to the bitter end,
quietly shedding their grief in piles
of silent tears,
mounds of leaves at their feet.
And then the wind took them
and scattered them over the hedges.

Jennifer Keevill

A DECEMBER GARDEN

I look out on the garden just what is it that I see?
Except a winter wilderness in all its finery!
The leaves are as bare as the ache in my heart -
Where love itself should be
As I stare out at the cherry tree
I picture you sitting there
Recollections of happier times
Spill out of what and when and where
And I *remember* your love for me!
Where does it go, this thing called love?
It's intangible and free
It only can be given, never taken - forcibly.
I am left with a sadness of soul
Amidst all this festivity
For I've spent my life with love as my goal
Now I face harsh reality
More and more I'm turning to the one above
Who always listens to me
And sends back down His love
In the beauty of a raindrop
In the radiance of a child
As we celebrate our Savour's birth
Pure love so undefiled.

Janet Robertson Jones

A WINTER LOSS

I know you will be there now
Now that winter's here
For never did a winter pass
But you appeared to cheer

I never needed to be told
That winter had arrived
A flash of red on garden fence
Heralded winter snow.

I am no longer there now
And miss you, little friend
Don't look for me to smile at you
From my glass kitchen door.

Opal Innsbruk

WINTER'S CONTRAST

The cosy fire, the soft glowing light
In contrast to the unforgiving night
The howling wind, the driving sleet
The pounding on the window as it beat,
Its icy shards upon the pane
This cold, unrelentless rain
Will it ever quieten, will it ever cease?

Then morning dawns, a quiet peace
The winter's sun plays across the land.
Her fingers reaching out, gently fanned.
The stark bare branches of the trees
Glistening, sparkling in the breeze
As night-time approaches and shadows fall
The birds sing out their evening call

The big yellow moon comes out to display
Its golden glow, its guiding ray
The Earth so bleak, so very bare
Gently transformed with great care,
Into a crisp white world, sparkling and bright,
In such contrast to the last, unforgiving night

Glenys Harris

SEASONS PASS

Who is it said
Gone are the halcyon days of summer
These words ring true
As now autumn leads
On into winter.
At last, the change
More gradual this year,
Letting us down gently
Into the chilly sombre colourings
By brightening them with soft
shafts of yellowy sun!
Into the icy coldness
By giving the illusion of warmth
Into the clear, fresh mornings;
Into the dark, dismal evenings
By letting the light stay a little longer
Until the altering of the clocks.

Yes, winter's here,
Summer and autumn have passed away
For another year,
And we look forward to a time
Of resting, dormancy and refreshing
Before spring comes bursting upon us!

Jane Otieno

EVERLASTING WINTER

Let there be no doubt
The cold out there is a
Reflection of the cold
In our hearts
I could have been
A better human being
But I chilled my heart
Hardened it and smote
The human race
We are all alike
Waiting to receive
A miracle to solve
The crisis of poverty
The chill inside breaks resolution
The frost numbs us
We numb our intelligence
Winter finally ends
But our negligence and ignorance
Go on and on in everlasting winter

Muhammad Khurram Salim

THE OAK AT HILLSIDE

So still she stands in all her majesty
Her gown, that was once the luscious green of summer,
Begins to turn all different hues
The sky unfolds yet another day of sunshine
Although late *October*
Giving out light fluffy clouds and brilliant blues
A gentle breeze rustles the falling leaves of this mighty tree
Making as if to whisper, winter is not far away!
The gold and reds, the amber tints, give out their beauty
For us to enjoy yet another glorious day.
The grass beneath her stately trunk,
Spreads out like a carpet at her feet.
Soon winter will strip her bare
Leaving gaunt black branches for us to meet,
What beautiful things are trees,
But for me, the oak surpasses all.
Each season may come and go from spring to fall,
But a thing of beauty she remains.

Edna Freeland

'TIS THE WINTER

When the sun is hidden by the thickening clouds
When rain has turned to snow
When the dew becomes like icing on a cake
When the cold north wind begins to blow
Then 'tis winter of the year.

When smiles and tender words no longer touch our lips
When voices raise and insults fly
When fault is found at every turn
When partners ask the question why
Then 'tis the winter of our love.

When pain invades the body and our memory departs
When we no longer plan ahead
When days and weeks go fleeting by
We think what happens when we're dead
Then 'tis the winter of our lives.

Robert Peirce

WINTER - WHAT IT MEANS TO ME

The highlight of winter, for me,
Has to be Christmas.
I look forward to it
Just as I look back to it
When spring appears.

The fading of Nature's green
Ushers in November,
A dull nondescript month
Source of fogs, rain, and early darkness
With but one redeeming feature -
Only 55 days till Christmas!

The wonder of hanging stockings
For Santa to fill, still endures.
I well recall my childish delight
On receiving the gift of a book
From a loved aunt. The story of 'Alice'
Enthralled me as I lived through each page
I have it still.

Scenes of Christmas still remain -
It always snowed!
We tramped in new Wellingtons
Down the country lanes, to sing our praises
At the village church - usually full in those days.

Today, at Christmas,
We keep the family around us.
It was always a special time,
A time for remembering the joys
A time to forget the sorrows
A time to give thanks for the love.

At the end of a memorable day
With the turn of the year close by,
My eager thoughts
Stride across the frosts of January
And the floods of February
To the beauty of the spring to come.
Winter quickly fades
In the rays of an April sun.

Beryl Louise Penny

WINTER

In the cold wet days, and days with snow,
When all the earth seems dead,
And there is nowhere for animals to go -
Unless they hibernate the whole of Winter, go without food.
When the last leaf has fallen from the sky,
And trees seem ghostly in their bareness,
Like arms reaching upwards to the heavenly high
But the only gift bestowed upon them is the frost and bleakness.

It is as though some fairy-like being
Has cast a magical spell, over all the surrounding land,
And every tree, bush and blade of grass
Have been frozen still, until the power of a magical wand,
Has brought all of life to Winter once more;
And slowly, the world of green, becomes a world of white.
Admire and see, the snowflakes fall,
Each one a kiss from Heaven, what a perfect sight!

Picture the setting, of snow white covered fields and glens,
Where the red deer run in herds.
And sheep who trudge in their thick woolly coats in the fens,
Huddle together from the icy blast.
But we, the humans, in the evenings sit indoors,
Warm, perhaps in front of a fire.
While icicles form outside on the windows and floors
And frost makes pretty patterns on the walls.

Winter, though it comes only once a year,
Brings about a crisp, white dressing,
To cover all the earth, it seems clear,
So all of us can make a new beginning.
When Spring at last does appear
And snow turns to waterfall,
How lovely are the coloured flowers
That ensure that Winter has gone, once and for all!

Hilarie Grinnell

WINTER'S TWIST

Blackened pansies in the garden
are a symbol of my fate.
When at last I knew I had loved
then it was just far too late.

Weary winds are softly blowing
through the crevice of my heart.
Bending, twisting, dropping, lifting
how I suffered for my art.

Vainly hoping, nothing telling
giving back what I can do.
Knowing nothing, but the hell in
which I have imprisoned you.

C Hullock

SPRING FANCY

Season of snowdrops and celandines,
Birdsong and loops of lilies;
Diamonds of dew form sparkling designs -
And we cast winter willies . . .

The sun warms its hands in readiness
To ring a peal of bluebells.
The first flowers add a headiness
To where tomorrow's view dwells.

The moist wind strokes the pussy willows,
Creep into homes where kittens
Make use of chair laid cushioned pillows,
And lick their lucky mittens.

When spring spreads her song sheet before us
Our hearts beat to the drummer time,
Glad voices swell the vibrant chorus,
A prelude to pre-summer time.

Bernard Shough

TAPESTRY OF SPRING

Mist and grey skies forgotten,
Nightingale songs echo
Where stone walls edge green fields.
A roughened trunk, dark and wrinkled,
Grows new curved branches, twisted together
In a tracery of patterns.

Pale almond blossom
Waves in sunlit patches
Framing clear skies,
Where white clouds float
And paths below
Are pink with drifts of petals.

Audrey J Roberts

SPRING'S DANCING SILVER LIGHT

Springtime shows us nature's wonders
All its glories on display
Thrusting life force eager fingers
Into each moment of each springtime day
After grey months of winter weather
Spring's sun bursts forth all warm and bright
Illuming all of God's creation
With rays of dancing silver light
So when you see the sunlight dancing
Through a new green leafy mantle shining
Shimmering there on breezes prancing
Like a fish's scales aglow
Watch a moving diamond blanket
With so many sequins shining
Reflected on the dewy earth below
Golden sun in all its glory
Created into patterns rare
Beauty in a space of seconds
Changing brightening here and there
Such embroidery, nature's wonders,
Cannot be the same again
'Cause leaves are growing breeze a blowing
Sunlight showing
Different shadows on the lane
Also in dells and wooded hollows
Bathed in dapples that are bright
All that sparkling glittering silver
Like a shower of Heaven's water
There drench yourself in speckled light
Then that energy reflected, will your human spirit raise
By sunlight that spreads and changes
In so many wondrous ways.

Ron Powell

SPRING-GREEN SPRUCE

New spring-green needles on the tips
Of upward curving branches to the crown
For eighteen years this Christmas tree has spread
And grown with topmost branches taking turns
To arc alternately like a ballerina's hands.

A Norway spruce in alien surroundings year on year
Where once a tiny potted evergreen
Was planted in suburbia on Twelfth Night
By teenage daughter number three
With great delight and pride and hope
As it survived and sprouted that first spring.

Now round the tattered skirts dog violets hide
Brushed by the needles from the earlier days
And bluebell generations come and go.

Once holly berries from discarded wreaths
Took root and produced crimson in their turn
A prickly dark green backdrop to the stage
Where on her pointed toes the dancer longs
To stretch yet higher towards the lightening sky.

Christopher Payne

Summer Dawn

It was a night of blue marble
clouds floated like cotton
across the moon
making isolated shafts of light
upon the water.

The sea was languid and lethargic
like a serpent at rest.
Lovers strolled hand in hand
touching their bare feet to the ocean
still cold with memories of winter.

Laughing like children
they ran along the sand.
Three o'clock,
the hour before the early summer dawn
the silence hung amazingly exquisite

It was like a solitary island
somewhere beyond,
where strands of light would
soon appear, like pink and gold ribbon
heralding the new day.

Kathleen Knight

SUMMER DREAMS

Golden footprints leading nowhere,
Circling in a wanton dance;
Blue, crystal sky awash with sunlight;
Magic setting for romance!
Rapturous ocean rushing onwards,
Competing with shrill seagulls' cry;
Glistening bodies paying homage
To their pagan god on high.

Summer dreams, like summer kisses,
Last but a moment, soon to fade
But in our treasure-trove of memories
These precious moments will be replayed.

Rosemary Thomson

A SUMMER MEMORY

Over the hills
ribboned rainbow
lost in rain;
in still green wheat
workers stood still

you, near me
naked in your sandals
on balcony, rain falls
scent of wood rises
mingling with bluebells

river floats
pale-green glacier
our boat waits in gloom
tied within willows' branches
current tugs it

still together
naked in boat
rushing through icy water
falls roar ahead of us
together, disappearing, boat gone

T Webster

SUMMER

Blue skies overhead
Music from a babbling brook
Green fields all around
Wild flowers everywhere I look
Garden full of honeybees
Scarlet dots of ladybirds
Ice cold drinks and strawberries
Chirruping of baby birds
Washing blowing in the breeze
Whistling husband early home
Children playing happily
Seaside treats are soon to come
Summer life flows easily
Household chores are quickly done
Then I read some poetry
While I'm lazing in the sun.

Beryl Williams

SUMMER'S SNAPS

I've received the snapshots today of a recent holiday -
Seen on the beach by the sea are pictures of you and of -
Who is he? It can't be me!
The person that I see must be at least 73,
That can't be me
There's a picture on the sideboard for everyone to see,
Now that is me.
He is maybe a little lighter, eyes a little brighter
He then, was me.
Thankfully, inwardly I remain as I used to be -
Relatively.
Seem to be just yesterday first saying precociously
That I am he.
But youth and maturity hastens into elderly
For all to see.
Mirrors show emphatic'ly - a vague similarity
Twix he and me.
Intrusively photography exposes the reality -
I'm not now he.
One is me at 23, t'other in antiquity
They could be me.
That image that I see must be at least 73
And he is me!

Stan Coombs

THE SUN

The bright relentless sun challenges man
To stand up and face its punishing rays.
Sun worshippers stand in its burning gaze,
Trying to soak as much glow as they can,
Spreading on lotion to maintain their tan.
Out in the hot sunshine they lie and laze,
During the holiday for many days,
Beside the pool waters of deep cyan.
The sun is so bright that it hurts the eye,
But we need it to make our planet thrive,
Without its rays we would certainly die,
But with far too much we would not survive,
I feel the hot sun blazing from on high,
This fine day makes me glad to be alive.

Gilly Jones-Croft

SUMMER IS ALREADY OVER

Summer is already over
In a world turned upside down,
For the breathy beat
Of digeridoo
And the desert heat
Of Uluru
I escaped an English winter
To a world turned upside down.

Summer is already over
In a world turned upside down
A rabbit replaced
The man in the moon
December weather
Was like our June
When I spent an English winter
In a world turned upside down.

My summer this year is over,
My life turned upside down,
Seasons exchanged
By a break I'd earned,
Life rearranged
Now I've returned.
My summer for this year's over
For I turned life upside down.

Geoff Hunter

SPRINGTIME

Free from winter's statement
Dormant life now resurgent
Re-mirror shape in parent form
Root pattern wriggle warm
With sympathetic worm weld
Free energy latent held.

Bud enlarging now burst through
Primitive look and colour new
Unabated slows to norm
Full shape set to given form
Colour radiant true hue glow
Tells spring's wondrous show

M P King

SUBMISSIONS INVITED
SOMETHING FOR EVERYONE

POETRY NOW 2004 - Any subject,
any style, any time.

WOMENSWORDS 2004 - Strictly women,
have your say the female way!

STRONGWORDS 2004 - Warning!
Opinionated and have strong views.
(Not for the faint-hearted)

All poems no longer than 30 lines.
Always welcome! No fee!
Cash Prizes to be won!

Mark your envelope (eg *Poetry Now) 2004*
Send to:
Forward Press Ltd
Remus House, Coltsfoot Drive,
Peterborough, PE2 9JX

**OVER £10,000 POETRY PRIZES
TO BE WON!**

Judging will take place in October 2004